NVIDIA Jetson Orin Nano Super

A COMPLETE Beginner's Step-by-Step Setup Guide

Mason J. Cole

Copyright © 2025 Mason J. Cole, All rights reserved.

No part of this publication may be reproduced, distributed, or transmitted in any form or by any means, including photocopying, recording, or other electronic or mechanical methods, without the prior written permission of the publisher, except in the case of brief quotations embodied in critical reviews and certain other noncommercial uses permitted by copyright law.

Table of Contents

Table of Contents..2
Introduction..4
Chapter 1: Understanding the NVIDIA Jetson Orin Nano..7
    What is the Jetson Orin Nano Super?...................... 7
    Key Features and Differences Compared to Earlier Models.. 8
    Applications: Generative AI, Local AI Servers, and Image Generation.. 14
    Recommended Hardware and Prerequisites.......... 15
Chapter 2: Preparing for Setup............................... 18
    Step-by-step guide to gather necessary items....... 18
    Preparing the microSD card................................... 23
    Optional hardware installation................................ 29
Chapter 3: Flashing the Operating System.............. 39
    Detailed guide to using Balena Etcher....................39
Chapter 4: First Boot and Initial Configuration........49
    Connecting Peripherals: Monitor, Keyboard, Mouse, and Ethernet... 49
    Setting Up the Jetson Orin Nano Super................. 51
    Introduction to the JetPack Operating System....... 55
Chapter 5: Running Local AI Models.........................58
    Overview of LLaMA and Local AI Hosting.............. 58
    Setting Up and Running LLaMA............................. 59
    Using OpenWebUI for a User-Friendly Experience 65
    Common Troubleshooting Tips for LLaMA

Installation and Interaction..68
Chapter 6: Exploring Image Generation...................71
Overview of Stable Diffusion....................................71
Setting Up Stable Diffusion Locally..........................74
Generating Images.. 79
Troubleshooting Installation Errors and Slow Performance.. 82
Chapter 7: Optimizing Storage with NVMe SSD...... 85
Configuring the NVMe SSD.................................... 85
Moving Docker Containers to the SSD................... 90
Testing and Confirming SSD Integration.................94
Chapter 8: Advanced Tips and Use Cases...............97
Using the Jetson Orin Nano as a Local AI Server.. 97
Understanding Power Modes and Performance Optimization... 104
Chapter 9: Common Challenges and Solutions.... 108
Conclusion... 118

Introduction

Imagine holding the key to unlocking cutting-edge AI capabilities right at your fingertips—a compact yet powerful device that transforms your wildest tech dreams into reality. The NVIDIA Jetson Orin Nano Super is more than just a piece of hardware; it's a gateway to a world where you can harness the magic of artificial intelligence without needing a supercomputer or a sprawling data center. Whether you're intrigued by the idea of running generative AI models, hosting your own local AI server, or diving into the creative realm of image generation, this device has the potential to be your ultimate tool.

This guide is crafted for those who might be curious but hesitant, eager but unsure. If you're new to AI or haven't dabbled in setting up complex systems before, you're in the right place. Maybe you've seen headlines about locally hosted AI or heard of LLaMA models, and the idea excites you, but the thought of actually getting started feels daunting.

You're not alone. This book is designed to strip away the intimidation and replace it with confidence, showing you step by step how to turn the NVIDIA Jetson Orin Nano Super into your personal AI powerhouse.

The setup process for a device like this may seem overwhelming at first glance, but when broken down into manageable, digestible steps, it's surprisingly straightforward. Each step is carefully explained, with clear guidance to ensure you don't feel lost along the way. By the time you finish this guide, you'll not only have your Jetson Orin Nano Super fully operational but also a solid understanding of its capabilities and how to make the most of them.

By the end of this book, you'll have learned how to flash the operating system, configure the device for peak performance, and explore its potential for hosting AI models and image generation. Whether you're setting this up for a personal project, exploring AI for the first time, or looking to add a powerful tool to your tech arsenal, this guide will empower you with the knowledge to take that leap. Turn the page, and let's embark on this thrilling journey together—because the only thing standing between you and your next big AI breakthrough is getting started.

Chapter 1: Understanding the NVIDIA Jetson Orin Nano

What is the Jetson Orin Nano Super?

The NVIDIA Jetson Orin Nano Super represents a breakthrough in compact computing, delivering unprecedented power and versatility in a single board designed to handle advanced artificial intelligence tasks. This device is part of NVIDIA's Jetson family, known for its ability to bring AI to edge devices with limited resources, making it ideal for developers, hobbyists, and enthusiasts alike. Despite its small size, it packs a punch, offering the ability to perform tasks that once required high-end servers or specialized hardware.

What sets the Jetson Orin Nano Super apart is its balance of affordability and capability. This iteration of the Jetson Nano series introduces features and performance enhancements that bridge the gap between accessibility and professional-grade computing power. Whether you're a beginner stepping into the world of AI for the first time or a seasoned developer looking to explore new horizons, this device opens up a world of possibilities. It's a playground for experimentation, learning, and innovation.

At its core, the Jetson Orin Nano Super is built for handling complex AI computations. It supports tasks such as natural language processing, image recognition, generative AI, and even real-time AI applications. Its adaptability makes it a perfect fit for developers seeking to create innovative projects or businesses looking to deploy edge AI solutions. As the demand for localized AI processing grows, the Jetson Orin Nano Super steps in as a device capable of keeping up with the needs of modern computing, while maintaining an approachable interface for those new to the technology.

Key Features and Differences Compared to Earlier Models

The Jetson Orin Nano Super introduces several notable improvements over its predecessors. These enhancements not only boost its performance but also expand its range of applications, making it a more appealing option for users across the spectrum.

1. Performance Boost

The Orin Nano Super is powered by NVIDIA's Orin architecture, which brings a significant leap in computational ability compared to earlier Nano models. It boasts up to twice the performance of the original Jetson Nano, enabling it to handle more demanding AI tasks with ease.

With upgraded GPU cores and support for higher memory bandwidth, it provides the computational power necessary for modern AI applications, from running LLaMA models to processing high-quality image generation.

2. Enhanced Performance with Firmware Updates

The Jetson Orin Nano Super owes much of its success to the firmware optimizations that accompany it. These updates ensure that the device runs efficiently, leveraging its hardware capabilities to the fullest. Firmware updates allow the Orin Nano Super to outperform earlier models in real-world scenarios, delivering smoother operations and faster processing times.

Boosted Computational Power

With firmware enhancements, the Orin Nano Super can achieve higher clock speeds and better thermal management, ensuring consistent performance even under heavy workloads.

AI models that would have previously slowed down older Jetson devices now run seamlessly, making it a reliable tool for developers pushing the boundaries of localized AI.

Simplified Updates

NVIDIA has made the process of updating firmware straightforward, ensuring users can stay current with the latest features and improvements. These updates can often be done with a few simple steps, minimizing downtime and maximizing productivity.

Backward Compatibility

For users of older Jetson models, firmware updates provide an opportunity to upgrade their devices without investing in new hardware. While they won't achieve the same performance as the Orin Nano Super, these updates extend the lifespan of existing devices.

3. NVMe SSD Support

The introduction of NVMe SSD support is one of the most transformative upgrades in the Jetson Orin Nano Super. By enabling high-speed storage solutions, this feature unlocks new possibilities for users, particularly those working with large datasets or running resource-intensive applications.

Why NVMe SSDs Matter

NVMe SSDs offer significantly faster read and write speeds compared to traditional storage solutions. This speed is crucial for AI applications, where loading large models and datasets quickly can impact overall performance.

The ability to use an SSD ensures that the Jetson Orin Nano Super remains responsive, even under demanding conditions.

Installation Options

The Orin Nano Super features two slots for NVMe SSDs: 2230 and 2280. These options give users flexibility in choosing the storage size and type that best fits their needs.

Installing an NVMe SSD is straightforward, and this guide will walk you through the process, ensuring even beginners can take full advantage of this feature.

Applications Benefiting from NVMe Storage

Local AI hosting: With fast storage, hosting AI models locally becomes more practical, reducing latency and improving responsiveness.

Image generation: Stable Diffusion and similar applications benefit greatly from the added storage capacity and speed, allowing for quicker processing times.

Development workflows: Developers working with large datasets or complex projects will appreciate the NVMe SSD's ability to handle heavy workloads efficiently.

4. Versatile Applications

Unlike earlier models that were primarily targeted at specific niches, the Orin Nano Super has broadened its appeal by addressing a wider range of use cases. From hobbyists exploring generative AI to professionals deploying AI solutions in edge environments, it caters to diverse needs.

5. Improved Ease of Use

With user-friendly tools and better integration with NVIDIA's software ecosystem, the Orin Nano Super simplifies the process of developing, deploying, and managing AI projects. Beginners and experts alike will appreciate the streamlined workflow it offers.

Applications: Generative AI, Local AI Servers, and Image Generation

The versatility of the Jetson Orin Nano Super makes it suitable for a wide range of applications. It serves as a bridge between accessibility and advanced functionality, enabling users to explore areas of AI that were once considered out of reach.

1. Generative AI

The device is capable of running advanced generative AI models, such as LLaMA, which allow users to explore natural language processing, text generation, and more. These models can be hosted locally, ensuring privacy and control over data.

2. Local AI Servers

With its ability to act as a local AI server, the Orin Nano Super empowers users to build and manage AI systems that are accessible across networks. This is particularly useful for collaborative projects or scenarios requiring decentralized AI processing.

3. Image Generation

Tools like Stable Diffusion make it possible to generate high-quality images on the Jetson Orin Nano Super. This opens doors to creative projects, from art and design to simulations and visualizations.

Recommended Hardware and Prerequisites

To fully utilize the Jetson Orin Nano Super, having the right hardware and tools is essential. Here's what you need to get started:

Computer

A computer is required to flash the operating system onto the Jetson Orin Nano Super. This will serve as your primary setup device.

MicroSD Card

A 128GB microSD card is the recommended minimum. For users planning to run large AI models or work with extensive datasets, a larger capacity card is advisable.

Optional NVMe SSD

While optional, an NVMe SSD is highly recommended for those looking to maximize the device's potential. The added storage capacity and speed will greatly enhance performance.

By ensuring you have these essentials, you'll be well-equipped to unlock the full potential of the NVIDIA Jetson Orin Nano Super and dive into its exciting applications.

Chapter 2: Preparing for Setup

Step-by-step guide to gather necessary items

Gathering the necessary items for setting up your NVIDIA Jetson Orin Nano Super is the first and most important step in unlocking its full potential. Having the right tools and software at your disposal ensures a smooth and efficient setup process, eliminating frustration and saving valuable time. This section provides a step-by-step guide to ensure you're fully prepared before diving into the actual configuration.

Step 1: Downloading the Jetson Operating System Image

The Jetson Orin Nano Super requires a dedicated operating system to function. NVIDIA provides an optimized operating system called **JetPack**, tailored specifically for Jetson devices. This OS is the backbone of the device, enabling its powerful AI capabilities and providing a user-friendly interface.

What is JetPack?

JetPack is a Linux-based operating system developed by NVIDIA. It includes everything you need to get started, from drivers and libraries to tools for running AI models. Think of JetPack as the Jetson's equivalent of Windows or macOS for a personal computer. (refer to *Chapter 4* for more*)*

How to Download the Jetson OS Image

1. **Visit the Official NVIDIA Developer Website**:
    - Go to NVIDIA's Jetson Download Center. This is the hub for all Jetson-related software.
2. **Locate the Latest JetPack Version**:
    - Look for the most recent version of JetPack compatible with the Orin Nano Super. Each update includes bug fixes, performance enhancements, and compatibility improvements.

3. **Download the Image File**:
   - Click on the appropriate download link. The image file will typically be a large .img file, often exceeding 10GB, so ensure your computer has ample storage space.
   - Save the file in a location that's easy to access, such as your desktop or a dedicated folder.

Tips for a Smooth Download

- Use a stable internet connection. Given the file size, interruptions during the download may result in corrupt files.
- Check the download page for any additional documentation or updates related to the JetPack version you're downloading.

Step 2: Software Required – Balena Etcher

Once you've downloaded the Jetson operating system image, the next step is to prepare the software needed to flash this image onto a microSD card. The recommended tool for this task is **Balena Etcher**, a powerful and user-friendly application designed for creating bootable drives.

What is Balena Etcher?

Balena Etcher is an open-source software tool that simplifies the process of flashing operating system images to storage devices. Its intuitive interface makes it an excellent choice for beginners, and it's compatible with Windows, macOS, and Linux.

(The Download and Installation steps are seen in *Chapter 3* of this guide.)

Step 3: MicroSD Card Considerations

The microSD card is a crucial component for the Jetson Orin Nano Super, serving as the primary storage medium for its operating system. Choosing the right card ensures optimal performance and prevents potential issues during setup.

Choosing the Right MicroSD Card

1. **Size**:
    - NVIDIA recommends a microSD card with a minimum capacity of **128GB**. However, for better performance and to accommodate large AI models, a **256GB card or higher** is advised.
2. **Speed Class**:
    - Look for cards labeled **Class 10** or **UHS-1/UHS-3**. These offer faster read and write speeds, which are essential for running AI applications smoothly.
3. **Brand Reliability**:

- Stick to reputable brands like SanDisk, Samsung, or Kingston. These manufacturers offer reliable cards with consistent performance.

Preparing the microSD card

Ensuring Proper Formatting

Preparing your microSD card for use with the NVIDIA Jetson Orin Nano Super begins with ensuring it is properly formatted. Formatting the card not only clears any existing data but also sets it up with a compatible file system, ensuring smooth performance when flashing the Jetson OS and running the device.

To start, verify the microSD card meets the recommended specifications. A capacity of **128GB or higher** is ideal for the Jetson Orin Nano Super, particularly if you plan to run resource-intensive AI applications or store large datasets. Additionally, the card should be labeled **Class 10** or

UHS-1/UHS-3, which ensures it can handle high-speed read and write operations without lagging during tasks.

Once you've confirmed the specifications, insert the microSD card into your computer. Most modern laptops and desktops include an integrated card reader, but if yours doesn't, you can use an external USB adapter. Make sure the connection is secure before proceeding.

For Windows users, open the **Disk Management** tool by right-clicking on the Start menu and selecting it from the options. Locate your microSD card in the list of drives, ensuring you've identified the correct device to avoid accidental formatting of other storage media. Right-click the card, select **Format**, and choose **FAT32** or **exFAT** as the file system. FAT32 is generally compatible across most systems, but exFAT is preferable for larger-capacity cards due to its ability to handle files larger than 4GB.

On macOS, you'll use the **Disk Utility** application. Open it from the Applications folder or Spotlight search, select your microSD card from the sidebar, and click **Erase**. Choose either FAT32 or exFAT as the format, and confirm the operation.

Linux users can format the microSD card using the command line. Start by identifying the device name using the `lsblk` command, then run `sudo mkfs.vfat` for FAT32 or `sudo mkfs.exfat` for exFAT. Ensure you input the correct device path to prevent formatting other drives accidentally.

After formatting, verify the card is completely blank and ready to accept new data. You can do this by opening the card in your file manager and confirming there are no residual files or partitions. If you encounter issues during formatting, such as the card being write-protected, check the physical write-protection switch on the side of the card or adapter, ensuring it's in the unlocked position.

Checking Compatibility with Your System

The microSD card you plan to use must not only meet the Jetson Orin Nano Super's requirements but also be compatible with your computer's card reader or adapter to ensure a seamless setup process. Compatibility issues can often arise from outdated card readers, driver conflicts, or improper connections.

Start by testing the microSD card with your computer. Insert the card and wait for it to appear as a connected device. If the card isn't detected, troubleshoot by:

1. Ensuring the card reader is functional. If the reader is external, try connecting it to a different USB port or another computer.
2. Checking for driver updates. On Windows, visit the Device Manager, locate the card reader under "Disk Drives" or "Universal Serial Bus controllers," and update the driver. macOS and Linux usually handle

drivers automatically, but if the card isn't recognized, ensure your operating system is up to date.

Next, verify the card reader supports the capacity and speed of your microSD card. Older card readers may not handle larger cards, such as 128GB or 256GB models, or higher-speed formats like UHS-3. If this is the case, consider upgrading to a newer reader or adapter designed for modern microSD cards.

Once compatibility with your computer is confirmed, test the microSD card for potential errors. Use tools like **CheckDisk (chkdsk)** on Windows or **Disk Utility's First Aid** feature on macOS to scan for and repair bad sectors. For Linux users, the `fsck` command can achieve similar results. Addressing errors at this stage ensures the card will function reliably during the Jetson OS flashing process.

By properly formatting and verifying compatibility, your microSD card will be ready to support the Jetson Orin Nano Super, minimizing potential issues during setup and ensuring optimal performance for AI and computing tasks.

Checklist for Necessary Items

To ensure you're fully prepared, here's a checklist of the items and tools required for the setup:

1. **Hardware**:
    - MicroSD card (128GB or higher, Class 10 or UHS-1/UHS-3)
    - USB adapter for microSD cards (if needed)
    - Computer with internet access and sufficient storage space
2. **Software**:
    - JetPack operating system image

- Balena Etcher for flashing the OS image
3. **Miscellaneous**:
   - Stable internet connection for downloads
   - A dedicated workspace to organize and perform the setup

With these items and preparations in place, you're now ready to begin the setup process for your Jetson Orin Nano Super. Taking the time to gather and organize these essentials ensures that the subsequent steps will go smoothly, allowing you to focus on unlocking the full potential of this remarkable device.

Optional hardware installation

Installing an NVMe SSD in your NVIDIA Jetson Orin Nano Super is a valuable upgrade that enhances storage capacity and improves overall performance. While it's optional, this hardware addition is highly recommended, especially for tasks involving large datasets, AI models, or image generation applications. The following walkthrough will guide you through the installation process and provide tips to ensure a smooth setup.

NVMe SSD Installation Walkthrough

Step 1: Understanding NVMe SSDs and Compatibility

NVMe SSDs (Non-Volatile Memory Express) are high-speed storage devices that connect directly to the motherboard through the M.2 slot. They offer faster data transfer rates compared to traditional SATA drives, making them ideal for AI applications that demand quick access to large files.

The Jetson Orin Nano Super supports two types of M.2 NVMe slots:

- **2230 Slot**: Accommodates smaller SSDs (30mm length).
- **2280 Slot**: Designed for larger SSDs (80mm length).

Step 2: Selecting the Right NVMe SSD

When choosing an NVMe SSD, consider the following factors:

1. **Capacity**: A minimum of 128GB is recommended, but 256GB or higher is ideal for AI workloads and extended storage needs.
2. **Speed**: Look for SSDs with higher read/write speeds (at least 2000 MB/s for optimal performance).
3. **Brand**: Stick to reputable brands like Samsung, Western Digital, or Kingston for reliability and warranty coverage.
4. **Form Factor**: Ensure the SSD matches the supported slot type (2230 or 2280).

Step 3: Preparing for Installation

Before starting, gather the following tools and items:

- The NVMe SSD of your choice
- A small Phillips-head screwdriver
- Anti-static wrist strap (optional but recommended to prevent static discharge)
- Clean workspace with proper lighting

Step 4: Powering Down the Device

1. **Turn Off the Jetson Orin Nano Super**:
   - Shut down the device completely and unplug the power adapter.
2. **Remove Peripheral Devices**:
   - Disconnect any attached peripherals such as keyboards, monitors, or USB devices to avoid accidental damage.

Step 5: Locating the NVMe Slots

1. **Flip the Device Over**:

- Place the Jetson Orin Nano Super on a soft surface to avoid scratching its exterior.
2. **Identify the NVMe Slots**:
    - Locate the two M.2 slots on the underside of the board. These are labeled for 2230 and 2280 SSDs.
3. **Choose the Slot**:
    - Decide which slot to use based on the size of your SSD.

Step 6: Installing the NVMe SSD

1. **Remove the Mounting Screw**:
    - Unscrew the small mounting screw at the end of the chosen slot and set it aside.
2. **Align the SSD**:
    - Hold the SSD at a slight angle (approximately 30 degrees) and align the notches on the SSD with the slot connector. This ensures proper orientation.

3. **Insert the SSD**:
   - Gently insert the SSD into the slot until it is firmly seated. You may feel slight resistance; this is normal.
4. **Secure the SSD**:
   - Press the SSD down until it is parallel to the motherboard. Replace the mounting screw to hold it in place. Avoid over tightening, as this may damage the board.

Step 7: Testing the Installation

1. **Reconnect Power and Peripherals**:
   - Plug in the power adapter and reconnect any previously removed peripherals.
2. **Boot the Device**:
   - Turn on the Jetson Orin Nano Super and check if the SSD is recognized by the system.
3. **Verify in the Operating System**:

- Use the JetPack OS or any terminal command (lsblk or fdisk -l) to confirm the SSD appears as a mounted drive.

Tips for Choosing the Correct Slot and Avoiding Installation Errors

Choosing the Correct Slot

- **Compatibility**: Ensure the SSD form factor (2230 or 2280) matches the slot you plan to use. Installing a mismatched SSD can damage the device.
- **Purpose**: If you plan to use multiple SSDs in the future, prioritize the larger 2280 slot for better storage options.

Avoiding Installation Errors

1. **Handle with Care**:

- Avoid touching the gold contacts on the SSD to prevent damage from oils or static electricity.

2. **Check Alignment**:
   - Double-check that the notches on the SSD align perfectly with the connector before inserting. Forcing an incorrect fit can damage both the SSD and the board.

3. **Avoid Over-Tightening**:
   - Secure the SSD firmly but gently. Overtightening the mounting screw can crack the SSD or damage the slot.

4. **Use Proper Tools**:
   - A small screwdriver with a magnetic tip is helpful for handling tiny screws. Avoid using makeshift tools that could slip and cause damage.

5. **Verify Firmware**:

- Some SSDs may require firmware updates to function optimally. Check the manufacturer's website for any available updates before installation.

Troubleshooting Common Issues

- **SSD Not Detected**:
    - Ensure the SSD is properly seated in the slot and the mounting screw is secured.
    - Check for compatibility issues between the SSD and the Jetson Orin Nano Super.
    - Verify that the firmware on the device is up to date.
- **Performance Issues**:
    - Use the NVMe diagnostic tools provided in the JetPack OS to assess the SSD's health and performance.

- Consider reformatting the SSD to a compatible file system if it isn't functioning as expected.

Installing an NVMe SSD may seem intimidating at first, but by following these steps and tips, you'll be able to enhance your Jetson Orin Nano Super's storage and performance capabilities with ease. This upgrade unlocks new possibilities for running resource-intensive applications, ensuring your device remains versatile and powerful.

Chapter 3: Flashing the Operating System

Detailed guide to using Balena Etcher

Using Balena Etcher to flash the Jetson OS image onto a microSD card is a straightforward process that simplifies setting up your NVIDIA Jetson Orin Nano Super. This detailed guide will walk you through downloading and installing Balena Etcher, flashing the OS image, and troubleshooting common errors during the process to ensure a smooth and hassle-free experience.

Downloading and Installing Balena Etcher

Balena Etcher is a powerful tool designed to create bootable drives, making it ideal for flashing operating system images onto microSD cards. Its user-friendly interface makes it accessible for beginners and advanced users alike.

Step 1: Visit the Official Website

- Navigate to the Balena Etcher website, https://www.balena.io/etcher/.
- Balena Etcher is available for multiple operating systems, including Windows, macOS, and Linux, ensuring compatibility with most computers.

Step 2: Download the Installer

- Choose the version that corresponds to your operating system:
    - For Windows: Download the .exe file.
    - For macOS: Download the .dmg file.
    - For Linux: Download the .AppImage file.
- Click the download link to save the installer to your computer.

Step 3: Install Balena Etcher

- **Windows**:
    - Double-click the downloaded .exe file to begin installation.

- - Follow the on-screen instructions to complete the process.
- **macOS**:
  - Open the .dmg file and drag the Balena Etcher icon into your Applications folder.
- **Linux**:
  - Make the .AppImage file executable by right-clicking it, selecting Properties, and checking "Allow executing file as program." Then, double-click the file to run the application.

Flashing the Jetson OS Image onto a MicroSD Card

Once Balena Etcher is installed, you can use it to flash the Jetson OS image onto a microSD card. This step is crucial for preparing the card to

41

function as the primary storage and boot drive for the Jetson Orin Nano Super.

Step 1: Prepare Your MicroSD Card

- Insert the microSD card into your computer's card reader or use a USB adapter if your computer lacks a built-in slot.
- Ensure the card has sufficient capacity (128GB or higher recommended) and is formatted to FAT32 or exFAT.

Step 2: Launch Balena Etcher

- Open the Balena Etcher application. Its clean and intuitive interface features three main options:
    1. **Flash from File**
    2. **Select Target**
    3. **Flash!**

Step 3: Load the Jetson OS Image

1. **Download the JetPack Image**:

- Ensure you've already downloaded the JetPack OS image from NVIDIA's official website. (refer to Chapter 2)

2. **Click "Flash from File"**:
    - Locate the .img file for the Jetson OS on your computer and select it.
    - Balena Etcher will verify the file and prepare it for flashing.

Step 4: Select the Target MicroSD Card

- Click "Select Target" and choose your microSD card from the list of available drives.
- Double-check that you've selected the correct drive to avoid accidentally overwriting another device.

Step 5: Flash the Image

- Click "Flash!" to begin the process.
- Balena Etcher will:
    1. Write the image to the microSD card.

43

2. Verify the written data to ensure accuracy.

- The entire process can take several minutes, depending on the size of the image and the speed of your microSD card.

Step 6: Safely Eject the MicroSD Card

- Once the flashing process is complete, Balena Etcher will automatically eject the card.
- Remove the microSD card from your computer and set it aside for use with the Jetson Orin Nano Super.

Troubleshooting Common Errors During Flashing

While Balena Etcher is designed to be user-friendly, issues can occasionally arise during the flashing process. Here are some common errors and how to resolve them:

1. Error: "Drive Not Recognized"

- **Cause**: The microSD card may not be properly inserted or recognized by the computer.
- **Solution**:
    - Ensure the microSD card is securely inserted into the card reader or adapter.
    - Try using a different card reader or USB port.
    - Reformat the card using a tool like SD Card Formatter and try again.

2. Error: "Image File Corrupted"

- **Cause**: The downloaded Jetson OS image file may be incomplete or corrupted.
- **Solution**:
    - Verify the file size matches the size listed on the NVIDIA website.
    - Redownload the Jetson OS image and select the new file in Balena Etcher.

3. Error: "Insufficient Space on Target Drive"

- **Cause**: The microSD card may not have enough storage capacity for the image.
- **Solution**:
    - Use a larger microSD card (128GB or higher recommended).
    - Check for hidden partitions on the microSD card and remove them using a disk management tool.

4. Error: "Flashing Process Stuck or Frozen"

- **Cause**: A software or hardware issue during the flashing process.
- **Solution**:
    - Close Balena Etcher and restart your computer before trying again.
    - Ensure no other applications are using the microSD card.

- Update Balena Etcher to the latest version from the official website.

5. Error: "Verification Failed"

- **Cause**: Data written to the microSD card does not match the source image.
- **Solution**:
    - Reformat the microSD card and repeat the flashing process.
    - Use a different microSD card or card reader.

Pro Tips for a Smooth Flashing Process

- **Check for Updates**: Always use the latest versions of Balena Etcher and the Jetson OS image for optimal performance.
- **Verify Downloads**: Use the checksum provided on the NVIDIA website to verify the integrity of the downloaded image file.

- **Avoid Interruptions**: Ensure your computer remains powered on and connected during the flashing process.
- **Test the Card**: After flashing, insert the microSD card into the Jetson Orin Nano Super and verify it boots correctly.

By following these detailed instructions and troubleshooting tips, you'll be able to flash the Jetson OS image onto a microSD card with confidence. This essential step sets the stage for powering up your Jetson Orin Nano Super and exploring its incredible capabilities.

Chapter 4: First Boot and Initial Configuration

Connecting Peripherals: Monitor, Keyboard, Mouse, and Ethernet

Before powering up your NVIDIA Jetson Orin Nano Super, ensure all essential peripherals are connected to streamline the initial setup process. These peripherals are critical for navigating the operating system, configuring settings, and interacting with the device during operation.

1. **Monitor**:
    - The Jetson Orin Nano Super uses a DisplayPort connection for video output. If your monitor supports DisplayPort, connect the cable to the device. For monitors with only HDMI inputs, you'll need a DisplayPort-to-HDMI adapter or cable.

- Ensure the monitor is powered on and set to the correct input source to display the output from the Jetson.
2. **Keyboard and Mouse**:
    - Connect a USB keyboard and mouse to the Jetson Orin Nano Super. Wired peripherals are straightforward to set up, but if you prefer wireless options, insert the receiver dongle into a USB port on the Jetson.
    - Test the keyboard and mouse functionality by moving the cursor or typing once the device is powered on.
3. **Ethernet**:
    - For network connectivity, plug an Ethernet cable into the Jetson's Ethernet port. While Wi-Fi is an option for later configurations, a wired connection ensures faster, more reliable internet access during the setup process.

Verify all connections are secure and functional before proceeding to power on the Jetson Orin Nano Super for the first time.

Setting Up the Jetson Orin Nano Super

Booting for the First Time

With all peripherals connected, you're ready to power on the Jetson Orin Nano Super. Insert the microSD card, flashed with the Jetson OS, into the device's microSD card slot. Ensure the gold contacts of the card face upward as you insert it until it clicks into place.

Connect the power adapter to the Jetson and plug it into a power outlet. The device will automatically power on, indicated by the activation of the onboard cooling fan and the display output appearing on your monitor. If the monitor remains blank, recheck the DisplayPort connection and ensure the correct input source is selected.

As the device boots for the first time, you'll see the Jetson boot screen, followed by the initial setup wizard. The wizard guides you through the essential configuration steps required to personalize and optimize the device.

Step-by-Step Walkthrough of Configuration Settings

Time Zone, Device Name, and Password Setup

1. **Select Your Time Zone**:
   - The setup wizard prompts you to select your time zone. Use the keyboard and mouse to choose the correct location. This setting ensures accurate timestamps for applications and system logs.
2. **Set a Device Name**:
   - Assign a unique name to your Jetson Orin Nano Super. This name is used

to identify the device on networks and during SSH sessions. Choose something simple and memorable, like "MasonCole01."

3. **Create a Password**:
    - Set a secure password for your user account. While a strong password is recommended, you can choose a simpler one for personal use. Ensure you remember the password, as it will be required for system access and administrative tasks.

Installing Default Browser and System Updates

1. **Choose a Default Browser**:
    - The setup wizard offers the option to install a web browser, typically Chromium. If you prefer another browser, like Firefox, you can skip this step and install your preferred browser later.

- If you opt for Chromium, the wizard will initiate its installation. Wait for the process to complete before continuing.

2. **System Updates**:
    - After completing the initial setup, the device may prompt you to check for system updates. This step is crucial to ensure the Jetson OS has the latest security patches, drivers, and features.
    - If prompted, connect to the internet via Ethernet or Wi-Fi and allow the system to download and install updates. This process may take several minutes, depending on the size of the updates.

Once these steps are complete, the setup wizard concludes, and the Jetson Orin Nano Super boots to the desktop environment, ready for use.

Introduction to the JetPack Operating System

JetPack is the official operating system for NVIDIA Jetson devices, including the Orin Nano Super. It is a Linux-based platform built on Ubuntu, customized to maximize the performance and functionality of Jetson hardware. JetPack provides a comprehensive environment for running AI applications, handling edge computing tasks, and developing innovative projects.

JetPack includes a suite of software tools, libraries, and drivers that enable the Jetson Orin Nano Super to function optimally. Key components include:

- **CUDA Toolkit**: Accelerates computation tasks, enabling efficient AI model training and inference.
- **cuDNN**: Optimizes deep learning operations for tasks such as image recognition and natural language processing.

- **TensorRT**: Enhances the performance of AI inference models, making applications faster and more efficient.

JetPack also includes development tools like SDK Manager, which simplifies the process of updating firmware, managing libraries, and installing additional software packages. The operating system provides a familiar Ubuntu desktop environment, making it accessible for users familiar with Linux.

The JetPack OS is designed to be versatile, catering to both beginners exploring AI for the first time and experienced developers building complex systems. It transforms the Jetson Orin Nano Super into a powerful yet user-friendly platform capable of handling tasks like generative AI, real-time object detection, and localized AI hosting.

With JetPack at its core, the Jetson Orin Nano Super becomes more than a piece of hardware—it's a gateway to cutting-edge technology that puts the power of AI in your hands.

Chapter 5: Running Local AI Models

Overview of LLaMA and Local AI Hosting

LLaMA (Large Language Model Meta AI) is a sophisticated open-source language model designed by Meta to perform various natural language processing (NLP) tasks. It is a powerful tool that allows you to generate human-like text, answer questions, translate languages, and more, directly from your local machine. By hosting LLaMA on your Jetson Orin Nano Super, you can leverage its computational power to run AI models locally, without needing an internet connection. This is particularly beneficial for use cases that require privacy, security, or low-latency processing, such as generating content, running local chatbots, and building AI-powered applications.

Local AI hosting using LLaMA allows you to run state-of-the-art models directly on your hardware, eliminating the need for expensive cloud services. This is especially useful when working with generative AI models that can demand significant computational resources. With the Jetson Orin Nano Super's capability to handle such models, you can maximize your local AI experience by integrating LLaMA into your machine learning workflows.

By setting up LLaMA locally, you gain complete control over the environment, which is ideal for research, prototyping, or developing AI-based solutions. You can fine-tune models, execute tasks more efficiently, and experiment without relying on external services.

Setting Up and Running LLaMA

Installing the Necessary Containers

Before you can run LLaMA on your Jetson Orin Nano Super, you must ensure that the necessary containers and dependencies are installed. Containers offer a lightweight way to deploy applications and software on the Jetson, allowing you to run LLaMA without worrying about managing complex environments manually.

1. Install Docker: Docker is the most popular containerization tool. To install Docker on your Jetson Orin Nano Super, open a terminal and enter the following command:

sql

Copy code

```
sudo apt-get update

sudo apt-get install docker.io
```

After installation, ensure Docker is enabled and started with:

bash

Copy code

```
sudo systemctl enable docker

sudo systemctl start docker
```

2. Download LLaMA Container: Once Docker is installed, you can pull the LLaMA container image from a repository. Meta may provide an official container image for LLaMA, but you can also explore community-supported options. In the terminal, run:

arduino

Copy code

```
sudo docker pull llama-image-name
```

Replace `llama-image-name` with the correct image name for LLaMA.

3. Run the Container: Once the container image is downloaded, you can start it by running:

arduino

Copy code

```
sudo docker run -it llama-image-name
```

This will launch the LLaMA model inside the Docker container, allowing you to interact with the model.

4. Set Up Dependencies: Some containers might require additional dependencies for full functionality, such as Python libraries or specific versions of TensorFlow or PyTorch. Ensure these dependencies are installed by checking the container documentation and running the appropriate commands inside the container.

Once the container is set up and running, LLaMA will be ready for interaction, and you can begin experimenting with its capabilities.

Running Basic Commands for Interaction

With LLaMA installed, you can now begin interacting with the model. The interaction typically happens via command-line prompts or APIs within the container environment. Here's how you can start:

1. Open the Container Terminal: If you've started the container, you should already be inside the terminal interface of the LLaMA container. If not, use the following command to access the container again:

bash

Copy code

```
sudo docker exec -it llama-container-name bash
```

2. Basic LLaMA Commands:

Start LLaMA: To start the LLaMA model and begin interaction, run:

Copy code

```
python run_llama.py
```

This command may vary depending on the container setup and script name. Consult the container documentation for the exact command.

Generate Text: To generate text, you can enter a simple command, like:

scss

Copy code

```
python generate_text.py --prompt "Your
text prompt here"
```

This will trigger LLaMA to generate a response based on the given prompt.

Model Configuration: You can modify the behavior of the model by adjusting parameters like temperature (controls creativity) and max tokens (limits the length of the response). For instance, you can run a command like:

css

Copy code

```
python generate_text.py --prompt "Tell
me a joke" --temperature 0.7
--max_tokens 100
```

Experimenting with these settings allows you to fine-tune the behavior and output of the LLaMA model based on your specific needs.

Using OpenWebUI for a User-Friendly Experience

Running AI models like LLaMA from the terminal can be daunting for some, especially beginners. A great way to simplify the process is by using OpenWebUI, a user-friendly web interface that lets you interact with the model through a browser. With OpenWebUI, you can access and manage the LLaMA model from a graphical interface, making the whole experience much more intuitive and accessible.

Setting Up the Web Interface

1. Install OpenWebUI: OpenWebUI can often be integrated into Docker containers or installed as a standalone service. To install it, follow the instructions provided in the OpenWebUI documentation. Typically, this involves downloading the necessary files and running the following command in your terminal:
bash

Copy code
```
git clone https://github.com/openwebui/openwebui.git

cd openwebui

python3 -m pip install -r requirements.txt
```

2. **Configure the WebUI**: After installation, configure the OpenWebUI interface by specifying which AI model to load. You'll generally need to set LLaMA as the backend model. This can be done through a configuration file or during the initial setup process of OpenWebUI.

Modify configuration settings such as the port number (e.g., port 8080) to ensure it doesn't conflict with other services running on your Jetson device.

3. **Start the Web Interface**: Once configured, start the web interface by running:

Copy code
```
python3 app.py
```

This will launch a local server, accessible through your browser by navigating to `http://localhost:8080` (or the port number you have set).

Accessing the AI Model Through a Browser

1. **Log Into OpenWebUI**: Open your web browser and navigate to the OpenWebUI interface. If this is your first time accessing the interface, you may need to sign in or configure authentication settings.
2. **Interact with LLaMA**: Once inside, the interface will allow you to input text prompts into a simple text box. After entering a prompt, the web interface will send it to the LLaMA model, which will then generate a response.
3. **Advanced Features**: OpenWebUI often provides advanced features, such as the

ability to save conversations, adjust model settings dynamically, or view logs. Explore these options to get the most out of your local AI hosting experience.

Common Troubleshooting Tips for LLaMA Installation and Interaction

While setting up and running LLaMA can be straightforward, issues may arise from time to time. Here are some common problems you may encounter and how to address them:

1. **Error: "Container won't start"**:
    - Solution: Ensure Docker is installed and running on your Jetson Orin Nano Super. Restart Docker by running `sudo systemctl restart docker`. If the problem persists, check Docker logs with `sudo`

`journalctl -u docker.service`.

2. **Model Crashes or Freezes**:
   - Solution: Running AI models requires significant resources. If LLaMA crashes or freezes, ensure your Jetson Orin Nano Super has sufficient memory and processing power. You may need to limit the model's parameters (e.g., reduce the maximum tokens or temperature) to prevent memory overuse.

3. **Unable to Connect to OpenWebUI**:
   - Solution: If you're unable to connect to the OpenWebUI interface, verify the server is running by checking the terminal for any error messages. Ensure that the correct port is open and accessible, and make sure you're navigating to the right URL in your browser.

4. **Slow Performance**:

- Solution: If LLaMA performs slowly, try adjusting the model settings. For instance, using a smaller model or reducing the number of tokens processed at once can help speed up interaction times. Additionally, ensure that your Jetson Orin Nano Super is connected to a stable and fast internet connection if required.

5. **Missing Dependencies**:
    - Solution: Ensure all necessary dependencies are installed by following the container's documentation or using a package manager like `apt` to install missing components.

By addressing these common issues, you can ensure a smooth experience while setting up and interacting with LLaMA on your Jetson Orin Nano Super.

Chapter 6: Exploring Image Generation

Overview of Stable Diffusion

Stable Diffusion is a cutting-edge generative model designed to generate high-quality images from textual descriptions, making it a powerful tool for artists, designers, and AI enthusiasts. It's part of the family of models known as *text-to-image* models, where users input a prompt, and the model generates an image based on the text description provided. The flexibility of Stable Diffusion lies in its ability to create not only photorealistic images but also abstract or stylized art, making it a valuable tool in creative industries.

Stable Diffusion has gone through several iterations, each improving upon its predecessors in terms of image quality, speed, and capabilities. The differences between model versions mainly come down to training data, model architecture, and hardware optimization. For instance, newer versions of Stable Diffusion are better at producing sharper, more coherent images, reducing artifacts, and handling more complex prompts.

Differences Between Model Versions and Hardware Requirements

Each iteration of Stable Diffusion has specific features and improvements over the previous ones. Here's an overview of some of the major differences:

- **Stable Diffusion 1.x**: The first versions of Stable Diffusion were impressive but had limitations in terms of image quality and the ability to handle complex prompts. They could generate basic images but often struggled with details in more complex scenes.
- **Stable Diffusion 2.x**: This version improved upon the architecture, producing sharper images and better handling of complex prompts. It introduced features like inpainting, which allows you to modify

specific parts of an image after it's been generated. The 2.x series also improved the model's ability to create images with more coherent compositions and less visual noise.
- **Stable Diffusion 3.x (and beyond)**: This version aims to provide even higher fidelity, producing photorealistic images with minimal artifacts. The advancements in the 3.x series further refine text interpretation, and it's optimized for use with more advanced GPUs.

When setting up Stable Diffusion locally on the Jetson Orin Nano Super, the hardware requirements can vary depending on which version of Stable Diffusion you intend to use:

- **Stable Diffusion 1.x**: This version can be run on less powerful hardware, making it suitable for systems with lower computational resources like the Jetson Orin Nano Super, though performance might be slower.

- **Stable Diffusion 2.x and beyond**: These versions require significantly more GPU power for optimal performance, which means that while the Jetson Orin Nano Super can still run these models, you might experience slower rendering times or need to tweak certain parameters for faster results.

The Jetson Orin Nano Super has the processing power to handle the lighter versions of Stable Diffusion (such as 1.x or 2.x with optimizations), but for more demanding models like Stable Diffusion 3.x, external GPUs or further optimizations may be needed to get smooth performance.

Setting Up Stable Diffusion Locally

To set up Stable Diffusion locally on your Jetson Orin Nano Super, follow these steps to install the correct container, prepare your system, and get the model up and running.

Downloading and Installing the Correct Container

1. Install Docker: Before you begin, ensure that Docker is installed on your Jetson Orin Nano Super. If not, refer to *Chapter 5* for installation process

2. Pull the Stable Diffusion Container: To get started with Stable Diffusion, you'll need to download the correct Docker container. Many versions of Stable Diffusion are available as pre-built containers, but make sure you choose the one that best fits your hardware. For example:

bash

Copy code

```
sudo docker pull stabilityai/stable-diffusion:latest
```

Make sure to check the container's documentation for specifics about model versions, system requirements, and any pre-configured settings that might be useful.

3. Run the Container: Once the container has been downloaded, you can run it by using the following command:

arduino

Copy code

```
sudo docker run -it stabilityai/stable-diffusion:latest
```

This will launch Stable Diffusion inside the container, allowing you to interact with the model.

4. Install Dependencies: If you encounter errors related to missing dependencies (such as Python libraries), follow the installation instructions in the container's documentation to resolve them. For instance, you may need to install additional libraries like `torch` or `transformers`.

Running Stable Diffusion Using Gradio Web Interface

The Gradio web interface provides a simple and interactive way to use Stable Diffusion without requiring you to run commands from the terminal every time. It's an excellent tool for beginners who want to easily input prompts and generate images through a graphical interface.

1. Install Gradio: Gradio is a Python library that allows you to quickly create a web interface for machine learning models. To install Gradio, run:
Copy code
```
pip install gradio
```

2. Configure the Web Interface: After installing Gradio, you can set it up to work with Stable Diffusion. Inside the container, create a Python script that loads the Stable Diffusion model and integrates it with Gradio. A simple script to get you started might look like this:
python

Copy code

```
import gradio as gr
from diffusers import StableDiffusionPipeline

# Load the Stable Diffusion model
model = StableDiffusionPipeline.from_pretrained("stabilityai/stable-diffusion-2")

def generate_image(prompt):
    return model(prompt).images[0]

# Set up the Gradio interface
```

```
iface                         =
gr.Interface(fn=generate_image,
inputs="text", outputs="image")
iface.launch()
```

This script loads the model and sets up an interface where users can type a prompt and see the generated image.

3. Launch the Interface: After running the script, Gradio will automatically open a web interface in your browser. You can now input text prompts and generate images directly from the Gradio interface.

Generating Images

Once Stable Diffusion is running locally through the Gradio web interface, you can start generating images. The following are some tips and best practices for working with the model to get the best results.

Basic Prompts and Best Practices

1. **Be Specific**: The more detailed and specific your prompt, the better the model can generate an accurate representation of your vision. Instead of simply entering "a dog," try something like "a cute golden retriever playing in a sunny park."
2. **Style and Composition**: You can include instructions about the style or composition of the image, such as "in the style of Van Gogh" or "photorealistic portrait." Stable Diffusion can understand and generate these types of requests fairly well.
3. **Experiment**: Stable Diffusion is very flexible, and you should experiment with different combinations of prompts to explore its capabilities. You can mix abstract and

literal elements, which can lead to unique and creative results.

4. **Negative Prompts**: Some versions of Stable Diffusion allow you to use negative prompts, where you can specify what you don't want in the image. For example, "no trees," or "avoid bright colors."

Example Scenarios and Limitations

- **Scenario 1: Fantasy Artwork**: If you want to generate a scene of a dragon flying over a mountain at sunset, your prompt might be:
"A majestic dragon soaring above a mountain range at sunset, with clouds and fiery orange skies in the background, highly detailed, fantasy art style."
- **Scenario 2: Product Design**: If you want to generate a realistic image of a new tech gadget, your prompt could be:
"A sleek, futuristic smartphone with a holographic screen, minimalist design, silver metal finish, and curved edges."

While the results can be impressive, there are certain limitations to Stable Diffusion:

- **Complex Scenes**: It can struggle with very complex or crowded scenes, such as large crowds of people or intricate architectural designs.
- **Details**: Fine details like faces, hands, and text may not always be perfect, and you might need to adjust the prompt or run the generation process multiple times.

Troubleshooting Installation Errors and Slow Performance

While setting up and running Stable Diffusion on the Jetson Orin Nano Super can be rewarding, it's not always a smooth ride. Here are some common issues you may encounter and how to troubleshoot them.

Installation Errors

Error: "Model Not Found": If you encounter an error stating that the model cannot be found, it may be because the model's path is incorrect or the model hasn't been properly downloaded. Double-check the model's name and path, and ensure that you've correctly pulled the necessary Docker container.

Error: "Missing Dependencies": Some dependencies may be missing after the container is launched. If this happens, follow the installation instructions to ensure all required libraries are installed. You can typically install them by running:
php
Copy code

```
pip install <missing-library>
```

Slow Performance

Optimize Resources: The Jetson Orin Nano Super may struggle with larger models, causing slow performance. Consider using smaller model variants, or optimize the settings to generate images faster, like reducing the number of inference steps or lowering the resolution of the output images.

Memory and GPU Usage: If the system runs out of memory, you may experience slowdowns or crashes. Monitor your system's memory usage using `htop` or similar tools and ensure that the GPU is being utilized effectively.

Chapter 7: Optimizing Storage with NVMe SSD

Configuring the NVMe SSD

The NVMe SSD (Solid State Drive) offers a significant performance boost, especially for resource-intensive tasks like running AI models, which require large amounts of storage and fast read/write speeds. Integrating an NVMe SSD into your Jetson Orin Nano Super setup can significantly enhance system performance, enabling faster data transfer, quicker model loading times, and an overall smoother experience when working with AI models like Stable Diffusion or LLaMA.

Mounting the SSD and Integrating It into the System

1. Connect the NVMe SSD: First, connect your NVMe SSD to the Jetson Orin Nano Super. If your system has an M.2 slot for NVMe SSDs, insert the drive into the appropriate slot. If you're using a

USB-to-NVMe adapter, connect the adapter to one of the USB ports on the Jetson device.

2. Check the SSD Detection: After connecting the SSD, you can verify that the system has detected the SSD by running the following command:

bash

Copy code

```
sudo lsblk
```

This will list all the storage devices attached to your system. You should see your NVMe SSD listed as something like `/dev/nvme0n1` or `/dev/sda`.

3. Partition the SSD: Before you can use the SSD, it needs to be partitioned. Use the `fdisk` command to create a partition on the SSD. Here's how:

bash

Copy code

```
sudo fdisk /dev/nvme0n1
```

In the `fdisk` prompt, press `n` to create a new partition. Follow the prompts to create a primary partition that takes up the entire drive. Once the partition is created, press `w` to write the changes to disk.

4. Format the SSD: After creating the partition, you'll need to format it with a filesystem. We'll use `ext4` for this example, which is commonly used in Linux systems:

bash

Copy code

```
sudo mkfs.ext4 /dev/nvme0n1p1
```

This will format the partition with the ext4 filesystem. The process may take a few moments depending on the size of the drive.

5. Create a Mount Point: Next, create a directory where you'll mount the SSD. For instance, you can create a directory called `/mnt/nvme`:

bash

Copy code
```
sudo mkdir /mnt/nvme
```

6. Mount the SSD: Now, mount the SSD to the directory you just created:

bash

Copy code
```
sudo mount /dev/nvme0n1p1 /mnt/nvme
```

To ensure the SSD is mounted automatically on boot, edit the `/etc/fstab` file:

bash

Copy code
```
sudo nano /etc/fstab
```

Add the following line to the end of the file:

bash

Copy code
```
/dev/nvme0n1p1 /mnt/nvme ext4 defaults 0 2
```

Save and close the file. This will mount the SSD every time the system boots.

Creating Directories and Assigning Permissions

Once the SSD is mounted, you'll likely want to create specific directories to store your AI models, Docker containers, or any other large files you plan to work with. It's important to ensure proper permissions are set for these directories to prevent any access issues.

1. Create Directories: You can create directories on the SSD where you want to store Docker containers, AI models, or other data. For example, if you want to create a directory specifically for storing AI models:

bash

Copy code

```
sudo mkdir /mnt/nvme/ai_models
```

2. Assign Permissions: It's essential to assign the correct permissions to these directories so that the Docker containers and other services can access and write data to them. If you're running the containers as a specific user (e.g., `jetson`), you'll want to ensure that the directories are owned by that user:

bash

Copy code

```
sudo chown -R jetson:jetson /mnt/nvme/ai_models
```

This will change the ownership of the directory to the `jetson` user, ensuring that all Docker processes and other applications running under this user can access the files.

Moving Docker Containers to the SSD

Using an SSD for storing Docker containers provides several benefits, particularly when running heavy workloads such as AI models. The faster read/write speeds of an NVMe SSD significantly reduce loading times, enabling more efficient data processing and quicker start-up times for containers.

Benefits of Using the SSD for AI Models

1. **Improved Load Times**: AI models can be quite large, and moving them to an SSD ensures they load faster into memory. This reduces waiting times when deploying or interacting with the models, providing a smoother experience.
2. **Better I/O Performance**: The NVMe SSD offers much faster data read/write speeds compared to traditional hard drives or even regular SSDs. This is especially useful when you're working with large datasets or running models that require frequent data access.
3. **Storage Capacity**: NVMe SSDs typically provide more space than microSD cards, which allows you to store more models and datasets without worrying about running out of space.

Step-by-Step Guide to Transferring Files and Verifying Setup

1. Stop Docker Containers: Before moving Docker containers to the SSD, it's best to stop any running containers to ensure data integrity:

bash

Copy code

```
sudo docker stop <container_name>
```

2. Move Docker Containers: Docker containers are typically stored in /var/lib/docker. You can move this entire directory to the SSD by first copying it over:

bash

Copy code

```
sudo cp -r /var/lib/docker /mnt/nvme/
```

3. Create a Symlink: After copying the Docker data to the SSD, you'll want to create a symlink (symbolic link) to point the Docker service to the new location:

bash

Copy code
```
sudo       mv       /var/lib/docker
/var/lib/docker.old

sudo   ln   -s   /mnt/nvme/docker
/var/lib/docker
```

This creates a symlink that tells Docker to use the new directory on the SSD. The `docker.old` directory can be safely deleted after everything is working correctly.

4. Restart Docker: Restart Docker to apply the changes:
bash
Copy code
```
sudo systemctl restart docker
```

5. Verify Docker Setup: Once Docker has restarted, you can verify that the containers are running correctly by listing all active containers:
bash

Copy code
```
sudo docker ps
```

Additionally, you can check the disk usage to confirm that the containers are now stored on the SSD:

bash
Copy code
```
df -h
```

This will show the storage utilization of your mounted drives and confirm that the Docker data is being stored on the NVMe SSD.

Testing and Confirming SSD Integration

After you've set up the NVMe SSD and moved Docker containers to it, it's essential to test and confirm that everything is working smoothly. Here's how you can test the SSD integration and verify that it's being used correctly:

1. Test Performance: Run a few AI models or containers that are resource-intensive and measure their performance. The SSD should provide a noticeable improvement in loading times and responsiveness.

2. Check Disk Usage: Run the `df -h` command again to ensure that the SSD is being used for Docker storage and that there are no unexpected issues.

3. Monitor System Logs: Check the system logs for any warnings or errors related to the SSD or Docker setup. Use the following command to view the logs:

bash

Copy code

```
dmesg | grep -i error
```

4. Verify Model Loading Times: For AI models, time how long it takes to load the model from the SSD and compare it with the loading time from the previous storage device (such as the microSD card).

The SSD should significantly reduce the loading time.

By following these steps and confirming that the SSD is properly integrated, you can ensure that your Jetson Orin Nano Super setup is fully optimized for running AI models and containers efficiently.

Chapter 8: Advanced Tips and Use Cases

Using the Jetson Orin Nano as a Local AI Server

The Jetson Orin Nano Super can serve as a powerful local AI server, allowing you to deploy and run AI models such as object detection, speech-to-text transcription, and more. By setting up your Jetson Orin Nano as a local AI server, you can leverage its GPU capabilities for AI inference and access it from other devices within the same network. This provides a flexible, cost-effective solution for running AI models locally without relying on cloud services.

Accessing the AI Server from Other Devices on the Same Network

To use your Jetson Orin Nano Super as an AI server that can be accessed from other devices on the same network, there are a few setup steps you'll need to follow.

1. Set a Static IP Address for the Jetson Orin Nano: By assigning a static IP address to your Jetson device, you ensure that it remains accessible from other devices on the same network. You can set a static IP address through the network settings:

- Open a terminal on your Jetson device.
- Edit the network interface configuration file:
  bash
  Copy code
  ```
  sudo nano /etc/network/interfaces
  ```
- Add a static IP configuration under the appropriate network interface section. For example:
  arduino
  Copy code
  ```
  iface eth0 inet static

  address 192.168.1.100

   netmask 255.255.255.0

   gateway 192.168.1.1
  ```

- Save the file and exit the editor.
- Restart the network service for changes to take effect:

bash

Copy code

```
sudo systemctl restart networking
```

Now your Jetson device will always have the same IP address on the network.

2. Enable SSH Access: Secure Shell (SSH) allows you to connect to your Jetson Orin Nano remotely from any other computer on the same network. Here's how to set up SSH:

- Ensure SSH is installed on your Jetson device:

  bash

  Copy code

  ```
  sudo apt-get install openssh-server
  ```

- Check the status of the SSH service:

  bash

Copy code

```
sudo systemctl status ssh
```

- If the service is not active, start it with:
  bash
  Copy code

```
sudo systemctl start ssh
```

- From any other device on the same network, you can SSH into the Jetson Orin Nano using the static IP address:
  bash
  Copy code

```
ssh jetson@192.168.1.100
```

Replace `jetson` with your username and `192.168.1.100` with the IP address of your Jetson device.

3. Web-Based AI Interaction: For an easier and more user-friendly way to interact with your local AI server, you can set up a web interface. For example, if you are running a model like Stable Diffusion or LLaMA, you can use a Gradio web interface or OpenWebUI. The web interface allows you to interact with AI models directly through a browser without needing to access the command line.

To set up a Gradio web interface, refer to *Chapter 6* for the process.

Now, from any device on the same network, you can access the Gradio interface by opening a web browser and navigating to:

arduino

Copy code

```
http://192.168.1.100:7860
```

Replace `192.168.1.100` with the IP address of your Jetson device. This will bring up the interactive interface where you can enter text, interact with the model, and see results in real-time.

Practical Applications and Examples

Using your Jetson Orin Nano as a local AI server opens up many practical applications, especially for edge computing and AI-powered systems that require fast, low-latency processing. Below are a few practical examples:

1. Object Detection: The Jetson Orin Nano can be used for real-time object detection using pre-trained models like YOLO (You Only Look Once) or SSD (Single Shot Multibox Detector). These models can detect and classify objects in video streams or images. For example, you could use the Jetson device to analyze camera footage for detecting faces, vehicles, or other objects.

To set up an object detection model:

- Download a pre-trained YOLO or SSD model from a repository.
- Install necessary libraries such as TensorFlow or PyTorch.
- Write or use an existing Python script to load the model, process incoming video streams,

and display the detected objects on the screen.

2. Speech-to-Text Transcription: With the Jetson Orin Nano, you can run AI models for speech-to-text transcription locally, turning spoken words into written text. This is useful for applications such as voice assistants, transcription services, or accessibility tools.

- Set up a speech-to-text model like Mozilla's DeepSpeech or the Google Cloud Speech-to-Text API (if you're working with pre-trained models).
- Capture audio through a microphone connected to your Jetson Orin Nano and send the audio data to the transcription model for processing.
- Display the transcribed text on the screen or send it to another application for further processing.

3. Edge AI for IoT Devices: The Jetson Orin Nano is perfect for IoT applications that require local processing of sensor data. For instance, you can connect the Nano to various sensors (temperature, motion, etc.) and run AI models to process the data and make decisions without needing to send the data to the cloud.

Understanding Power Modes and Performance Optimization

One of the most important aspects of using the Jetson Orin Nano Super is optimizing its power consumption and performance. Since AI workloads can be demanding, ensuring that your Jetson device operates efficiently without consuming unnecessary power is crucial for maintaining a balance between performance and longevity.

1. Power Modes: The Jetson Orin Nano comes with several power modes that help manage energy consumption. These modes adjust the device's performance based on workload demands.

- **Max Performance**: This mode runs the device at its highest performance level, ideal for demanding AI tasks. However, it consumes more power.
- **Power Save**: This mode reduces the power consumption, which can be useful when the device is idle or running lighter tasks.
- **Custom Power Mode**: For more specific use cases, you can set a custom power mode to balance performance and energy efficiency based on your needs.

To check and configure power modes, you can use the `jetson_clocks` utility:

bash
Copy code

```
sudo jetson_clocks
```

This will ensure that your device runs at maximum performance, especially when running resource-heavy tasks.

2. Performance Optimization: To optimize the performance of your Jetson Orin Nano Super, consider the following best practices:

- **Use Hardware Acceleration**: The Jetson device has a built-in GPU that can accelerate AI tasks. Make sure to use libraries like TensorRT or cuDNN that are optimized for the GPU to maximize the inference speed.
- **Optimize Your Code**: Ensure that your AI models are properly optimized for edge devices. Use quantization, pruning, and model distillation techniques to reduce the model size and increase inference speed.
- **Monitor Resource Usage**: Use tools like `nvidia-smi` and `tegrastats` to monitor the CPU, GPU, and memory usage of your Jetson device. This will help you identify bottlenecks and make adjustments as needed.

bash
Copy code
```
nvidia-smi

tegrastats
```

3. Thermal Management: AI workloads can cause the Jetson device to heat up. Make sure that your device is placed in a well-ventilated area, and consider using a heatsink or fan to keep the temperature under control. High temperatures can lead to thermal throttling, which reduces performance.

By following these power and performance optimization techniques, you can ensure that your Jetson Orin Nano operates at peak efficiency while handling demanding AI workloads.

Chapter 9: Common Challenges and Solutions

Setting up the Jetson Orin Nano Super can be a rewarding experience, but like any complex technology, errors and roadblocks are common during the setup process. Many beginners will encounter issues, and understanding how to resolve these problems is key to ensuring a smooth setup. One of the most frequent issues faced is when the OS image fails to flash onto the microSD card. This can manifest as the Jetson Orin Nano Super not booting, or displaying an error during the boot sequence. The cause of this can be a corrupted OS image file, a faulty or low-quality microSD card, or an incorrect flashing process. To solve this, ensure that the image file being used is the correct and latest version from NVIDIA. If in doubt, redownload the OS image from the official source. Additionally, using a high-quality microSD card (Class 10 or UHS-1, at least 128GB) can prevent this issue. If the flashing process still fails, consider re-flashing the OS image using Balena Etcher or a similar tool, carefully following the flashing steps to avoid mistakes.

Another issue that users commonly face is the Jetson Orin Nano Super failing to boot after the OS image has been flashed. This issue can sometimes be linked to improper peripheral or power supply connections. It is important to double-check the connections of peripherals such as the keyboard, mouse, and monitor to ensure they are properly connected. Sometimes, the failure to boot could also be due to a low-power supply. The Jetson Orin Nano Super requires a stable power supply (5V 4A) to function properly. If underpowered, it may fail to boot. In this case, using the correct power adapter is crucial, and testing the setup with another adapter could be beneficial if you continue to experience booting issues.

Another common challenge is getting the system to connect to a network, whether it's via Ethernet or Wi-Fi. After booting, some users may find that the

Jetson Orin Nano cannot connect to the internet or local network. This issue often stems from misconfiguration of network settings or a lack of proper network drivers. The first step is to ensure that network settings such as IP addresses are correctly configured. If you are using a static IP, make sure it does not conflict with other devices on the network. In some cases, restarting the network services can resolve connectivity issues. You can do this by entering the following command:

bash

Copy code

```
sudo systemctl restart networking
```

If the issue persists, checking the Ethernet cable and router connections is important. If you're using Wi-Fi, make sure that you have entered the correct Wi-Fi credentials during the setup process. A connection failure could also indicate that the router itself needs attention or that a particular setting in the router is preventing the device from connecting.

Another issue that some users face is the monitor not showing any output. This could be due to a range of factors including a faulty HDMI cable, an incorrectly connected cable, or an incompatible monitor. If the Jetson Orin Nano Super is not displaying anything on the monitor, try re-checking the cable and ensuring that it is properly connected at both ends. Sometimes, switching to a different monitor can help rule out compatibility issues. Additionally, if using other video output modes like DisplayPort, ensure that the system is set to use HDMI, as the Jetson Orin Nano Super may default to a different output mode depending on the configuration.

Occasionally, errors can arise when running AI models or installing software packages, particularly if dependencies or libraries are missing. This is common when working with AI models like

LLaMA, Stable Diffusion, or object detection models. The software may throw errors about missing dependencies, which could prevent the model from running as expected. To resolve this, ensure that all necessary dependencies are installed. For example, you might need to install frameworks like PyTorch, TensorFlow, or TensorRT, depending on the AI model you're working with. These can be installed via package managers such as `pip` or `apt`. It's also important to verify that the NVIDIA Container Toolkit is properly set up if you're running models within Docker containers. The toolkit allows the Docker containers to access the GPU for better performance. You can install the toolkit with the following command:

bash

Copy code

```
sudo apt-get install nvidia-container-toolkit
```

Once the dependencies and containers are properly configured, the AI models should function without error.

Avoiding common pitfalls during setup can greatly enhance the experience for beginners. One of the best practices for those new to the Jetson platform is to read the documentation thoroughly. NVIDIA provides detailed setup guides and instructions that can prevent issues before they arise. These documents cover everything from OS installation to hardware configuration and software installation, offering clear guidance at every step. Rushing through the setup process without fully understanding the instructions can lead to frustration and errors.

Another tip for beginners is to start with simple projects before diving into complex AI models. The Jetson Orin Nano Super is a powerful device, but it's wise to build up experience with basic projects first. Try running pre-trained models such as object detection or simple image classification before attempting to set up more complex AI models like generative models or custom setups. These simpler tasks will help you become familiar with the system's environment and performance.

Also, make sure to avoid cheap or low-quality microSD cards. The performance of the Jetson Orin Nano Super is heavily dependent on the quality of the storage device you use. Low-quality cards may result in slower boot times, crashes, or even data corruption. Always choose a high-speed, reliable microSD card, preferably one with at least Class 10 or UHS-1 ratings, and 128GB or more in storage capacity.

Keeping the software up to date is another best practice. NVIDIA frequently releases software and firmware updates that fix bugs, improve performance, and add new features. To ensure your Jetson Orin Nano Super is running optimally, check for updates regularly. Updating your software also helps with security, ensuring that any vulnerabilities are patched. You can update the system by running:

bash

Copy code

```
sudo apt-get update && sudo apt-get upgrade
```

For beginners, using pre-built Docker containers for AI models can save a lot of time. These containers are optimized to run on the Jetson platform, saving you the headache of configuring each software dependency manually. NVIDIA and the AI community provide containers that are ready to go, allowing you to get started quickly with minimal setup.

Maintaining the Jetson Orin Nano Super also involves regular cleaning and optimization. As your system grows with more models, data, and software, it's easy for unused files to accumulate. Regularly clean the system by removing old models or packages you no longer need. You can use tools like `apt-get autoremove` to remove unnecessary packages. Additionally, ensure that your storage, particularly if you're using an NVMe SSD, is well-managed to keep the system running efficiently.

Lastly, be mindful of system cooling. AI models and high-performance computing tasks can cause your Jetson Orin Nano to generate a lot of heat. If the system overheats, it could throttle its performance or even cause hardware failure. Invest in adequate cooling solutions like heatsinks or fans to keep the temperature within safe limits. Keeping the system cool will ensure it continues to run at its best.

By following these tips and practices, you can prevent common errors and pitfalls while maximizing the performance and longevity of your Jetson Orin Nano Super. Troubleshooting is an inevitable part of working with advanced technology, but with the right approach, most issues can be resolved quickly and effectively.

Conclusion

As you've journeyed through this guide, you now stand at the threshold of unlocking the true potential of the Jetson Orin Nano Super. What began as a series of steps—downloading the OS, flashing the microSD, connecting peripherals, and diving into the world of local AI hosting—has transformed into a powerful foundation for your AI exploration. But this is just the beginning.

You've now set up a sophisticated AI system that will open doors to limitless possibilities. Whether you're running complex generative models, creating local AI servers, or delving into cutting-edge applications like image generation, speech recognition, or object detection, the Jetson Orin Nano Super is your gateway to building something extraordinary. Remember, the path you've taken is one of curiosity, experimentation, and growth. This device is more than just a tool—it's a platform for innovation, and what you do with it next is entirely up to you.

But don't stop here. As you've seen, the capabilities of the Jetson Orin Nano Super extend far beyond the confines of this guide. The world of AI is vast and constantly evolving, and your Jetson device is a living, breathing part of that progression. Keep pushing boundaries, and continue exploring the endless potential of this powerful little machine. Dive deeper into the world of LLaMA, experiment with Stable Diffusion, push the limits of image generation, and perfect your local AI hosting setup. There's so much more to discover, and with every experiment you run, you're not just learning—you're innovating.

To help you continue on your journey, there are countless resources at your disposal. Online communities, forums, and official NVIDIA documentation will be invaluable as you navigate new projects, troubleshoot issues, and share your breakthroughs with others. Platforms like GitHub, Stack Overflow, and even dedicated AI forums offer endless support and inspiration. Embrace these tools as you refine your skills, because the more you learn, the more you will realize just how much there is to explore.

Take full advantage of the opportunities that come with the Jetson Orin Nano Super. As you grow and experiment with more advanced AI techniques and projects, you'll find yourself contributing to a larger community of AI enthusiasts and creators who are reshaping the world. Whether it's generating stunning visuals, advancing speech-to-text technologies, or running AI models in real-time, you've now got the tools, knowledge, and power to be part of this revolution.

So, go ahead—unleash your creativity. Let your imagination guide you as you continue to explore, experiment, and push the limits of what's possible. The Jetson Orin Nano Super is not just a device; it's the start of something bigger. The questions you have today will evolve into the answers of tomorrow. Keep learning, keep building, and above all, never stop experimenting. Your adventure has only just begun, and the future is yours to shape.

Made in United States
Orlando, FL
27 April 2025